Swimming the Eel

Swimming the Eel

Poems by Zara Raab

David Robert Books

Published by David Robert Books
P.O. Box 541106
Cincinnati, OH 45254-1106

Typeset in Garamond by WordTech
Communications LLC, Cincinnati, OH

ISBN: 9781936370443
LCCN: 2011934916

Poetry Editor: Kevin Walzer
Business Editor: Lori Jareo

Visit us on the web at www.davidrobertbooks.com

Cover art: Water color by Judith Nelson
Author photo: Andrea Young

Acknowledgments

"A Bride's Questions," "Grasses," "Infidels of Light," "Social Studies," "Swimming the Eel," "Tanning," and "Yellow Fields" appeared in *Song of the San Joaquin* in 2006 and 2007.

"April 18, 1906 in San Francisco," *Arts & Letters*, vol. 13, Spring 2005.

"Artemis in the Barnyard," *Sin Fronteras*, 2010.

"Awake Now," *Manzanita: Poetry & Prose of the Mother Lode & Sierra*, vol.5, 2006.

"Billy Gawain," *Evansville Review*, 2011.

"Deliveries," *Aurorean*, Fall/Winter 2008.

"Dust," *Manzanita, Poetry and Prose of the Mother Lode*, 2010, ed., J. Holzer, M. Rose.

"Earthquake Weather," *Spoon River Poetry Review*, 2010.

"Eclipse," *Eclipse*, 2010.

"Gravel-Man" and "Winter Wheat," *Marin Poetry Center Anthology* 2007.

"Hogback," *The Dark Horse*, 2011.

"Interstates" and "Meditation on Flying," *Santa Clara Review*, vol. 97, no. 1, Winter Spring 2010.

"Landscape with Snakes," "Coyotes," and "Two Crops," *Nimrod International Journal*, 2009.
"Landscape" was also anthologized in *The Place That Inhabits Us*, Sixteen Rivers Press, 2010.

"Mendocino Co.," *Vintage Voices: Words Poured Out*, Redwood Writers' Club, 2010.

"Oscar," *Monterey Poetry Review*, vol. 3, no. 1, Spring 2007.

"Paper Route," *Carquinez Poetry Review*, no. 4, 2006.

"Snake in the Grass," *Third Wednesday* 2010.

"Stitch," anthologized in *Lavanderia: A Mixed Load of Women, Wash, and Word*, ed. by Donna Watson, Michelle Sierra, and Lucia Gbaya-Kanga (San Diego: City Works Press), 2009.

"Trees of Harvest," *EDGZ*, no.5, 2003.

"Trionesta," *Magnolia: A Florida Journal of Literary and Fine Arts*, Issue 4, 2010.

"Wild," *River Styx*, 2011.

"Whiskey," *Red Line Blues*.

"Yoga," *Dos Passos Review*, 2009.

"Dog Creek," "Cochrane Street," "Deposition No. 12," "In the Pear Orchard," "Exile," "Fishing the Eel," "Herring Gull Variations," "Main Street," "Social Studies," and "Walking in Humboldt County" all appeared in the Summer issue of *Third Wednesday*. "Cochrane Street" also appeared in *Song of the San Joaquin*.

Contents

For Nadia and Benjamin, always

I

A Land of Wonders

Winter Wheat

—Illinois, early 1800s

The furrowed earth turned, sown to
bluestem wheatgrass, the roots mined
six feet down in pantaloons of
soil along the river rock.

Up and down the hot cornrows
the seeds of winter were strewn,
till under the snowy sod,
the new wheat began to move,

and the wind howled and westward
the chiefs of Black Hawk rose like
black storm clouds preparing to
spend themselves on their own ground,

ravines of the Fox and Sioux,
pastures of the Chippewas,
till the grass roots turned to rust,
and titled escrows turned to

blooded mares and thoroughbreds,
driven west along the trail,
in their turn scattered and lost,
or traded for snow and bread.

Traces

Beyond memory
but for this photo,
melancholy man—
Alonzo—
the vowels catch like earth
on roots upturned
on Old Misery.

Restless, the orphaned
ward of Algonquin
wives, you headed West
to California,
Don Alonzo de Calvin,
walking the Lost Coast,
slipping from memory.

Little stirs there now
but fescue grasses.
Loosened from the bone,
still, your name cascades—
Alonzo—
the pollen of oak
across yellow fields.

Once

Once there were two brothers, Don Alonzo and Frank
Hand, born in the early 1840's on a homestead outside
Dubuque, Iowa. Swarthy, said to be Black Irish,
descendants of sailors from the Spanish Armada gone
aground on Irish soil during a storm, they were restless
young men, each going his own way, not in a wagon train,
but as bachelors do, solo, ever westward.

What drew the brothers West? Long before they set out
on foot and horseback their eyes walked among the word-
trees planted by writers of the West, word-trees planted
with pen and watered with ink and imagination. Their
dreamy eyes were lost in seeds of grass in that "land of
wonders" called California.

Goodly Tents

By dark, he'd got as far as the Lolo
running out of Bitterroot, where the Salish
hunting grounds still hummed with arrows.

Along the Lolo, Russian olives,
gifts of other travelers, languished,
sending to the river their bitter missives.

Their gray leaves shimmered in the dark.
Night fell, open air banished
by a well-joined roof of stars.

He rigged a makeshift tent and slept
in the woolen weave his mother Eve
had given him—now frozen stiff, a tent

of cloth off the rump of his filly.
His breath a furnace to the room, he
slept at last, and woke to trees

of green. If I were this man, I'd be
content to settle down, but he's young
and brash, and follows a filigree

of trails heading West from the Lolo
across deserts as far as Eden.
In those valleys his voice still echoes.

Shelter Cove

1

Our rituals
are walking, sapling-siblings,
from Shelter Cove to the Mattole,
to our tall, grizzled great-uncle's
winter wheat fields barely topside,
walking and skirting the shoals below
the old light house, that, and racing
the rising tides.

Oak trees
cluster inland by the laurel,
by the springy, pungent pine-boughs
for our bedding, Eel Kakonee
for our meals; mile on mile, we tread
the beach to the cedar house,
Knowles', the uncle we hardly know,
the homestead.

Oak's a wattle
of leaf whose branches lean
over Knowles' fields their green, tough
leaves; there graze his cattle.
Tufted like cow's ears, those leaves,
forming a crown that dips and soughs,
but will not fall in oak's reign—
a hundred years.

2

We felt an ease,
children playing Geronimo,
getting by, need be, on grandpa's
red-brown acorns—fruit of the tree—
the hard, turtle-shaped loaves
made from a fresh, warm *nup'-pah*
of mush dipped into some cold,
secluded cove.

I'm no believer—
still, with the speed of days passing,
old, I sometimes think I still know
God's hands, his palms holding me,
while down the valley time rolls,
inexorable as Knowles'
plan for heifers penned for branding
beside the Mattole.

Oak's a tree
of simple need, rain for taproots
whose crown years on we wore
at Knowles' grave in that valley
of the shadow not far from home,
will wear again the day we roar
un-penned at last from our chutes,
branded to bone.

Whiskey

In the hollows of lightning-struck trees,
deep in the forest of the Wiyots,
the fathers ran their stills when you were
still a boy by the cold-running Eel;
they hid the cucurbit of berries,
the mash of scented, fermenting grain,
and lit their secret flames below, then
by every hook and crook jury-rigged
a rick for aging the casks of gin.

Blessed be these makeshift alembics
passed down to you—all else there was oath
and curse, every half breath a "damn it,"
or "hell," so thank God, thank the Scotsman
for the waters of life that cleanse you,
the *usquebaugh*, the bourbon whiskey,
raw as salt searing the quenched throat,
turning to vapor all troubles,
de-fanged an evening and slow-content.

Old Sally James

Born in a thimble of rye,
sloshed and hung out to dry,
I live a life, transpires
in its own blessed time,
fermenting in me
this brew of poetry.

Easy I slip into sleep,
drowsy in the dyer's heat.
That or I'm all a-startle,
my ideas abstract,
missing the simplest fact,
at odds with rational acts.

With a curve in my spine,
I tumble walleyed
in love, sock in a dryer,
rushing, getting nowhere,
cycling in regular loads,
hot to warm, cool, cold.

My yen's a trunnion,
carriage loaded and wrung.
I can't go home 'cause
my taw's disappeared,
my only means there
a red-nosed reindeer.

Fishing the Eel among the Athapaskans

To the place of the Athapaskans
Tom Buhe came for salmon that ran
spawning the Pacific
where three Wiyot elders were weaving
their nets and stitching the casing.
One motioned with his stick.

In his hip boots, Tom went to him
through fescue grasses high as his shins,
shouldering his creel,
two men standing where Eel fell to sea,
the Wiyot at home in their tipis,
Tom with his lines and reel.

Week by week the summer green bled
from the grass as the salmon spread
splendor through the river.
Casting out, Tom caught seven salmon
in hues of tangerine, almond,
apricot and silver.

The Wiyot praised them in Athapaskan,
but said, "Let's follow the bracken,
seaward past the quicklime."
The sun was setting; their pace was slow,
day winding down; for the Coho,
too, a swallow of time.

Tom trailed after the ancient Wiyot,
the wind blew and the white caps
greeted the Wiyots who wove.
He shivered, "It's cold and growing late.
Upriver my tired father waits
by a pinewood stove."

Just as the sun pierced the bloodroots,
the tide swamped him, filling his boots,
releasing his foothold.
Though wild, flailing like memory lost,
thrashing a way out of chaos,
the drowned quickly go cold.

No ferryman waited with solace,
only eelgrass in deep forests
quickly set caressing.
No pines waited on the Eel's far shore,
only kelp on the ocean floor
among sea worms glowing.

Tides rolled over Thomas like a cloud,
where old Wiyot bones were plowed,
the Yurok, Karuk, and Hupa.
They mingle in the mouth of the Eel,
turning, turning as on a wheel
the Whilkut, Chilula.

High, high above the shore's barren rocks
spin the herring gulls, gannets and auks.
Tipis have all perished.
Beside them swam the spawning salmon
in their iridescent titian.
Coho, too, have vanished.

Belle and Mary

Bachelors need wives in order to thrive, and Alonzo was no exception. A wife was coming to him; even as he was heading west, she was making her way there by another route, one of two sisters sailing from Augusta, Maine on a 5,000-mile voyage to California a few years after the Civil War. First stop was New York harbor, where they boarded the *California*, traveling third class for $375 in dirty, cramped quarters, traveling with men who spat and swore and scratched their unshaven chins and their crotches. After many days and one six-knot gale, they arrived in steamy Panama, pesthole of the world. Here on a dismal, hot midday in February, they disembarked at Aspinall, and they spent the night in a mosquito-infested hotel. In the morning, they boarded a train bound for Panama City, where they put up in another grimy hotel, taking their meals in the café downstairs, waiting for a north bound clipper ship to take them up the West Coast to San Francisco.

At last, on a mild spring day, Belle and Mary arrived at San Francisco's harbor. On the pier stood their mother and a man Belle hardly recognized, but knew must be her father. Beside them stood a younger man, perhaps sixteen, who smiled at the girls and took their bags. Fate and character and a hundred people and events took the two sisters on different paths. Mary stayed home, and later married a prominent citizen and lived her life in a stately Victorian in the center of town. Belle? She had tasted adventure. What was it Belle discovered on board the *California*? Mary was too young to remember much of the voyage, but Belle was on the cusp of womanhood the night a storm struck the *California*, water rushing into the hold where the girls slept in hammocks slung from a rafter. She would never forget what happened that night. It shaped her and reshaped her through the years, the way tides and storm shape a beach. Just four years after Belle disembarked from her sea adventure, at sixteen, she set off on another adventure of a rather different kind.

Stitch

(*Bear Creek, 1880*)

Sewing is lyric.
Back and forth, my hand
conducts, transforming
red and blue flannel
into shirts, working
my own stitch in time
for the coming winter,
for the hard chill to
fall on the mill camps
up and down the coast
where lumber jacks turn
in their makeshift cots
and wait for rain to stop.

On certain evenings
I follow the thread
to the time of Ice:
stitch by stitch I see,
lying in embers
of straggling fir,
a slender bone, pierced
at one end, severed
from the foreleg of
an arctic fox or
the red doe's pelvis,
bone useful then for
picking and scratching.

Across a million
odd years the cold chills
my Bear Creek cabin,
and so, my hand still

scoring my thoughts,
I take up rawhide,
or a strand of my hair,
and thread the pierced bone,
suturing seams of
deer, bark, or mammoth—
tailoring breakers
against ice and wind.

Hands

O mouth, what would you do without hands to feed you,
without the stubby thumbs pulling back from fingers?
Where would you live, O mouth, without these two hands
who make line by line and stick by stick the lodge, the
shack, the place to bivouac beside the night body?
Hands did not draw the cave with its shape like yours,
mouth—No, hands had no part in shaping that maw—
except perhaps to make fists or bombs that may yet drive
us back there, to caves, to sit before their raging fires.

Infidels of Light

She got up, the ghost of herself, when her
father called, his voice a bark in the night.
Small and pale, with a shock of red hair, she
shivered, and gulped the coffee in her mug,
then climbed up to the high seat of the wagon,
and they rode together, saying little.
Her breathing calmed, thoughts rose and fell
like clouds moving unobserved in the dark.
They rode out into the fields of yellow
grass at the end of a dusty, rutted
road, bumping along until night slackened
Its pace before the infidels of light.
If they killed a buck, there'd be much to do—
skinning him and gutting the viscera,
shiny with blood—she could slip off awhile,
a day at the river—O, what pleasure!
Day began to spread—a rush of warm light
ahead, like the sight of land from the sea.
Her father took the rifle from the truck
and began walking. They hadn't far to go
before they saw the buck standing among
trees at the distant edge of a field.
She had the first shot—sure, she was a girl,
but her aim was pure and nearly perfect.

Christmas

Advent brought rain, slicking
the roads and dimming
light over the valley,
wrinkling the old face
of the earth into gullies;
in town, lights burned
over the transoms
and in the Yule trees;
the Mattole spilled its banks,
shimmered through gray,
washing away the dead
in Honeydew and Fern.
When rain paused, smoke
broke from our rooftops;
on hills, red cedars
fattened till Spring,
when axe and saw would
fell them one by one.
At home, we fattened
on Porter House rolls,
and stole looks at gifts
tied in bright string
by the lit balsam.
Where would elves go
once the alders were cut?
Raining cats and dogs
that Christmas stained
a deeper black the black spruce
neat-stacked in the mill yards,
and on the mire paths, no stars
were seen, but whose footfall
was it in the dinning rain?

Wild

We glimpsed them from inside the wire mesh
of the cool sun-porch, the bristled spines,
dun-streaks of some rippling the dusky air,
others with the lumbering gait of bruins:
sounder of dark, farrowing sows streaking
Mendocino sedge. Once beasts of hunting,
or figures of blasphemy and ruin,
nothing stops them, grizzled and stiff-haired
on the unruly homesteads, not woodbines,
not fences, not even the waist-high rush.

One night we caressed, a huge male passed.
I was fifteen then; we lay concealed
by grass and heard him snorting and rooting
with his long sharp tusks, eager to dig out
the hawkweeds and gorge on bristly carrot
and too-ripe fruit. His sows would be fattening
soon come the autumn in the yellow fields
where white-tailed deer startle and bound.
For creatures tamed or traded, wildness is
only lying fallow, waiting, blameless.

Alonzo

Alonzo Hand stood on the San Francisco pier when Belle
and Mary stepped off the *California*. He fell in love with
Belle, and when she was a little older, they married. On
horseback, the two youngsters—sixteen and twenty—set
out for Bear Creek. It would be many years before Belle
would see her sister again. At Bear Creek, Alonzo built a
one-room log cabin in a draw of the valley. Their first child
was soon born and Alonzo built another cabin just east of
the first, with two rooms and a fireplace but no running
water. A child was born every two or three years. The
family lived in the two-room cabin until the oldest child
was thirteen, and could help his father build a big, two-
story, eight-room house with glass windows down near the
fork in the county road. *"The lumber for the house was hauled in
from the forest nearby, sawed in the sawmill built by Father,"* his
youngest son remembered, *"The bricks for the fireplace were
shipped from Port Kenyon."* This house became known as
"greater downtown Hand." It was a one-room school, a
post office, as well as the family home. Belle was Post
Mistress, Alonzo delivered the mail.

Belle

"There [at Bear Creek]...the first twelve years of her married life have been spent, and this is her first return visit. This we call pioneering. This is the courage, the fortitude, which is displayed by those who go before and open a new country to civilization..."

—June 16, 1883.

Infantry, too, precede the engineers,
cavalry, and generals— those at the rear.
Infantry's the war's niggers, I am told.
I, too, am black—with tar and soot and dirt,
or red from insects and stinging nettles
and sunburn in the fields by the Mattole.
We can't take land that belongs to itself—
infiltrate the lines of chiggers and tarweed,
a thousand batteries of leaf and bug.
Nameless spiders, lizards and snakes outrun even the
smallest claim made by us.
In fields of battle, stench is uppermost
though I should not name it. Here every dawn
I'm greeted by it in the milking barn,
again in the henhouse Alonzo built.
Now the creek a dozen feet off runs brown.
Like an acorn, against all the odds,
I take root where no tree shades the ground.

Belle Hand

1

When I was seven
I set sail from Maine,
and on the seventh night, my soul
left me while a sailor dreamed
in his swinging bedroll.

That night my soul flew off
like a seabird tossed
windward to the girls and sailors
drowned at sea or lost
in soul as I was that summer.

Did my poor soul
recognize the small bowl
beneath my heart, and find
when I was ten a porthole
of return in time?

2

Does the Spotted Owl
have a soul? Do my cows
lowing, milk-heavy, in their stalls?
Do mosquitoes?
My weary body, too, calls

on waking for its soul.
As I pass the fox's burrow
beneath the pines just before dawn
and slip on mossy stones,
suddenly alert, I pause:

Through trees there's a glimmer
of the moon, a tremor
of Douglas fir branch settling
an owl into its arms,
the sudden, light sting

of nettles as I brush
against a bush in my search
for mushrooms and wild berries.
Is my soul the solace
of my sensual body?

A Bride's Questions

How will I keep the damp away when fog hugs the coast?
If rattlers bite, will you mark time till I die?
How long to fetch the doctor?
Will you kiss me if I smell of earth and goats?
Who will boil water when my labors come?
Will my child wear shoes or the leather of his soles?
When the rains begin, will the henhouse
grow mold and kill my chicks?
Will the fire die and fill the room with smoke?
The creek is cold, how will the boys wash?
Once the mites and lice begin to live with us there will be no divorce.
How will I keep deer from my corn?
How will we pass the from dusk to dawn?
What story will we tell, once we've kissed,
braised each inch of skin with lips and hands?
When will I see again the dressmaker?
my sister? the ships coming to harbor?
And if I wake in the night—but I will not.
I will not. I will sleep or I will lie awake,
my tongue hugging the roof of my dry mouth until morning.

Pine Trees

The pines grow bored with mountains,
wind whistling in the quarry,
making rute of needles.
Yet they are loyal, steadfast,
indifferent to vainglory:
They let wind tease and wheedle.
When I see their simple grace,
can I mind *my* sad story?
Spring comes, and pine's there, bustling.
Do they yearn for the seaside?
They seem to rise against wind,
but wind blows through them, rustling.
It moans *Who are you?* to them.
Still they stand like bowling pins,
lined on the crests of valleys.
Though once legion in this place,
a handful still bowl and spin
their cones along the gullies.

Alonzo's Mother

Bear Valley, 1880

She had left much behind, now it was spring
her seventy-eighth on earth, her second
in the West, in the *Mattole* whose waters
fed the tall grasses, and she was strangely
moved by the grassy hills sloping seaward.
At night, she slept and dreamed of a stallion
cantering to her across the coastal plain,
then—huge, distended—standing over her.

In the morning, when she walked the prairie
through a veil of fescues and hair grasses,
satin tail and sedge arching over her
in moving fountains, she hid for a time
signs of frailty—the sagging breasts, pouches
of skin beneath her chin and eyes, even
her thinning hair—she drowned them in seas
of gold-flowering California grasses.

In the first rains of autumn, the grasses
spring up lime green; by summer they turn
dusty white, but just now they're delicate
rods of gold, binding the soil, resisting
a short while the tide of wind and water,
and stirring creatures to life each morning.
Eva moves through seas of grasses at dawn,
and she is one with them, rustling, stirring.

Hogback

The blue Chevy with the windows down
is his idea of indoors, summers;
he has the spine and walk of hogback,
his bones the dark and coarse-grained basalt;
his stained, half-missing fingers fisted
over the wheel, he cusses, and pulls
the trigger on a harem of does,
(and misses) downwind in the tare grass,
then roars into third so's to bypass
thinning pinewoods and ferret the coves
for three braces of pearly mollusk.
He's a jack-of-all-trades. Come sundown
to the lit sawmill, he'll strut around,
trimming the burl and burning the husks.

His new woman stands by the oven
of her gold-dun kitchen, baking rusks,
she's a girl of the wide open fields,
home in fescue and tare and chickweed.
Sundays, while he jaws the venison,
she's yet to rev the Chevy's engine,
or sight along a twenty-two,
she'll come along, he says, none too soon.
This very morning she took her knapsack
to the blue-lupin pastures, loony
as a bluebird among the dobbins,
and in due time, she'll mount the hogback,
track bucks with points on the knobby spine,
and shoot to kill, too, and not soften.

Gravel-man

"The world was mine, sometimes I ground it to just
the size I needed, the size of peas, the bits of
gravel for my roads: Rock and bone and shell,
stone, nail and horn—I ground them all to pebble—
harvest for the sediment of freeways,
the white sands gleaming on either side.
Voices, too—the sounds of laughter or words—
inquiries or suggestions—yours or mine:
I tossed them up. I ground them with my heel.
Even the vision of the blue beech arched
over the veranda being set then with
lawn chairs and serving trays of lemonade—
even the whiffs of your perfume or my diesel
couldn't reach me, enthroned near the sun, when
I set out to take up the paving of highways."

Yellow Fields

Our own mother was a small town girl, dark
and slim, unschooled, artless, and big-hearted—
who kept a clean house over a green hill
and mothered us four children. That's all—
until the day she unwound the turban
of home and ran out bareheaded, leaving
us for dreams, for the Idea of Love.
Small town life had turned stale and boring.
We had turned stale and boring. She wanted out.
She wanted the new life she dreamed of *now*,
quick, she threw wide open the doors of her
cell, and walked out into the yellow fields.
She didn't consider having to spin
her powers to God, she didn't reckon
the waterfall of loss, how its pounding
muffled the sounds and scents all around her.
Head bare, she walked out into the open,
where the deer step at twilight, ears twitching,
Upwind of the hunter's scent, the scent of
powder in the guns, and of grass burning.

Winter Cord

He dreamt of flying, of infants tumbling
like towhees through the air—
and woke to see her feeding their child.

He rose, washed his hands, and went out,
scouting for over-growth and setting
the sap-sticky saw-teeth to bite.

Air churned, dust scattered. From the shack,
she could just hear the crackling
and splitting of wood—a long day's work,

a summer song for winter wood.

Tanning

His father showed him how to strip the bark
from the father tree of oaks, and lay it
in long wooden crates, the tanbark staining
the boy's hands the color of the Yahi—
tannin *Algerian* to sweeten leather—
exposing the taproots of his body.

The oaks had already lost their bright leaves.
They lay scattered over the winter ground
in that valley of comfort and shadow.
The summer shade of the massive boughs
traded with the darker shade of winter
circling the cold fields in peaks of snow.

The boy came from those vistas, stripping the
skin of oaks already stripped of their leaves.

San Francisco Earthquake

Agnew State Insane Asylum
San Jose, California, April 18, 1906

Small trees surrounded the asylum, bending
blossoms to us at dawn, bathing us in spring
in milky fragrance—our bodies seeming
completely innocent of feeling, our minds
detached, clear. Round and round we swam
in our tub of dreams, white clouds tumbling
down to the rock-black, sand-white shore.
When the walls broke to the shuddering earth
and a woman ran out, carrying her baby
like a trussed chicken, and *Caruso* stood
at the open window, at the opera before him
as he sang out, *"La fanta mi salva
l'immondo ritrova"* to those standing half
nude in sleep's dance by the fallen porticoes—
even then, trees were rooted in their bodies,
alive, sleeping, old as the oldest living thing,
standing, sturdy as grocers or rabbis,
stretching up their limbs, as the earth shook,
and the orderlies removed their suspenders,
caught us by the wrists, and tied us to them.
Leaves flapped and whirled, blossoms powdered
and lathered our missing faces.

White Pine

Even now the trees speak: they tell
how all these years we spread
our pine boughs by the Mattole
where Pomos and Yahi bed
by cracked flints and arrowheads.

We trespass the farmer's groves,
gleaning pippens for the deer.
At dusk, does and their young move
from the woods to pasture where
we feed them; they have no fear.

I eat the wild orchard's fruit;
Tree on tree gives peach and plum.
The pine lack fruit we can eat—
only for itself the cones.
I take these, too, with my thumb.

II

Coming to Branscomb

Grandfather's grandfather

Grandfather's grandfather was an ardent Abolitionist in
Kansas, assassinated while buying tobacco in the general
store. Great-grandfather Benjamin signed on with the first
wagon train coming through Kansas from Missouri, a train
led by a craggy old man who took Benjamin on as a hired
hand. They arrived in California in the late summer. Like a
puppy, Benjamin followed the wagon master's beautiful
daughter, and soon married her. They had many children,
and when the youngest was eight, they packed up and set
out for a homestead in the Jackson Valley, a remote place
in the north coast. Veterans of the War were already there,
shell shocked or crippled, bedraggled and worn, all a little
crazy scraping by on their government pensions. These
pensions arrived in the little metal mail boxes of the post
office where the post mistress was Nell, Benjamin's
daughter-in-law, the only one in the family of her
generation to arrive late, by train, to this promised land.

Billy Gawain

(1895)

We'd been traipsing the long afternoon
through the bramble, when we came upon
him hanging from the oak, his black boots
almost scraping on the ground, bowing
down a branch half-cleft from the oak's crown.
His hands seemed to take back what he'd done,
they at least had wanted life, clawing,
frantic to unknot the fraying jute,
his thick, blackened nails cut and bloodied.
Now the arms hung loosely at his side.

His trousers were stained dark in the crotch,
the eyes in his ancient face held watch
on the air where the black crows circled.
I'd never seen a body before,
cut down and laid out in the stinkweed.
He had no kin, so he was buried
with our own, the only name he bore
the name we gave him and had chiseled
on his headstone at the spring solstice:
"Billy Gawain, A Stranger to Us."

Deposition No. 12

My great-great-grandpa was a gung-ho
Abolitionist, I'm proud to say,
a Civil War soldier in Kansas
shot coming out of the General Store
by pro-slave bandits, so goes family lore.
When his strong-willed son didn't
take to someone, he recalled his
forbears, and up and left, going west
in a wagon when he was young and then
in middle age north to the Jackson Valley.
He had a passel of children by then,
my grandpa—eight or nine—-was one
who said his father drove them like oxen
to plow and plant, weed and hoe that land
a stone's throw from the Pacific Ocean.
Grandpa learned to read with his kin
in one room—such narrow company
can drive a person a little crazy,
I'll testify to what such a life can do;
back then there was no one else around
but a few Civil War pensioners
and the big, brown Yahi who skated
barefoot on the Eel when it froze solid.
The Yahi boys, too, kept to themselves
for their fathers recalled too well
the Yankees of generations gone,
their pitch and *got-to-be-this-way* zeal.

Nellie

(1910)

She traveled as far as the Pacific
in a wagon drawn by horses and dreams,
the pollen rising in the dewy air—
until she stood beside the Eel where
wild plums were first to flower in spring,
the meaning of a journey orphic
to the blossoms singing in white-pink
where she stood, in due time becoming
a watershed before the flood, before
the draught that was surely coming,
for times when the earth would close,

when rain would die and white clouds gather
and give nothing but beauty to the air.
Still, apples blossomed and flowers—blue,
yellow, orange—set fire to meadows.

No, She Said

By his side, she lowers her eyes
and feels the rapture she knew as
a child racing Sue and Eunice
the whole of Vine Street in distant
Trionesta. In this new place
steep and narrow streets run constant
to the warp and woof of earth
and twine below where steamers berth.

Above hills, a white moon rises,
the same moon her yearning sisters
watched rise and set, and breathless,
she hears them in her ear, whisper
as she gazes out, hand on her cheek.
He touches the wisps on her nape,
and traces the curve of her neck;
she turns to the darkening seascape

and stirs—but then over her
a sudden, lunar tug washes
and to her solitary ground
she withdraws as dusk comes down;
lamps are lit in terraced houses
standing sentinel by the harbor.

You Never Know

Does it matter that I did not
once see him after we dallied?
My longing almost ceased; I took
myself off like that and married.

Twenty-seven years, I've thought
of him, the boy so lightly attached,
the barber's son who once went out
for coffee and never came back.

Yet he stayed behind in the East,
while I rode West on the Northern line.
Listening for tunes on the CB,
I got word of him from time to time.

By "if and only if," logic
means business, but my own mantra
"You never know" or "What if. . ."
means "if I were in Trionesta."

Now my life has passed in Branscomb,
and while the past is not present,
at my age, the past is often home,
neither past nor absent.

Even as a young girl, I'd brood—
not like my loose-limbed sister, Belle,
haunting scarred streets laid down like roods.
I, too, once told the lovers' tales.

The pleasures we shared! So I sigh,
humming the morning aria
we shared, the barber's son and I
in the streets of Trionesta.

Going to Branscomb

She set out alone in March; winter had filled
the pools over the old flows of lava,
mold grew in wisps along the fallen logs,
waves of orcuttia grasses rooted in the mud
     and sent out their bitter stalks.

Litters of leaves squirming with centipedes parted
a wagon width, a rutted path along the ridge.
Water was already scarce: she forded the Eel
at Branscomb, hoe rattling in the wagon,
     and claimed her land at last.

By July, lizards overran the ground; hyssop
died by the scarlet poppies. Even so, orcutt
flowered in the cracked earth; cocks across
the way at Branscomb engendered chicks at dawn
     just by cock-a-doodling.

Nell's First Year

In spring, we walked the Elder by alder
and elk's clover all the way to the sea,
teal and gray, and skirted there the tangled
strands of coppery seaweed, the blind eel.

Real as any creatures, no more so, we
sought no talisman, only the tufted goats
feeding among the oaks, only the phoebes
streaking the air, and the cool northern slope.

In winter, the sun's arc to the sea begins
at four, as the sky darkens into dusk.
Soon night comes, opening my soul to dreams.
Until then, I move through my house,

shuttering all the windows, then knead
the dough for a strudel of summer pears,
and lay his nightshirt on the upstairs bed.
I fluff the pillows; my bridegroom comes near.

Deliveries

(December 18, 1921)

Pregnant again, her fourth, the post mistress
of Branscomb stood facing the metal slots,
backsides flipped back, tiny doors alight,
though any day her labors would move up
the narrow road to the big snow-white house
set deep in the land of the Sinkyone.

She knew the stirrings on the spine, the slight
muscle-tensing, the current of waiting,
of walking on blind feet through the warm silt.
Reaching, she drew a handful of letters,
one by one studied their codes, the scrawls,
the flourish, the neatly penned—watching

for post from Jamestown, Bradford, or Kane.
She held the towns as her mother had done,
once, past, in the little house in Erie:
Hoping for word of Sraid an Mhuilinn, Cork,
borne in the dark, slippery hold of a ship,
steaming across the cold, vast Atlantic.

Coyotes

Who'll join me in this room
as the winter séance
starts, wind rattling the pots?
My girls, bending their heads
over their murmuring dolls?
The Sinkyone, whose bones,
deep under the floorboards,
shift and turn in the dark?
The gingerbread men I
shape, as my mind drifts off?
Who now living or dead?
I've been content these years,
my household a refuge,
secure from solitude;
I still hold the world off;
not so much as peering out
after a passing truck,
engine coughing to life
beneath rolls of thunder.
But today I'm restless.
Now my son bangs the door
on his way to the barn.
I follow his blurred form
through the rain-streaked glass,
but soon lose him; I lose
the thread of the girls' talk
and find myself, instead,
thinking of the coyotes
in the hills, their calls beating
the ground, as I thump the dough.
This rain firing like B-Bs,
they have hunkered down
as we have until spring.

Oscar

(1925)

Not the tail-wagging beagle who followed her
everywhere in the fields off Laurel Street—
spotty, floppy-eared, who later took up
sheep rustling, not the black and white pug,
round-cheeked and -bellied, smelly, mouth
dripping, rear wriggling—no, this was Oscar,
the marigold-colored mutt who, the day
she sat splay-legged by the nasturtiums
on the summer veranda, trotted up
from fields of corn and when she started up,
sprang and bit—hard—her upturned face,
spilling the blood that sent waves through her,
along the dress she wore, her sister's dress,
the one already red, now red again
in each seam stitched by the mother's hand.

Swimming the Eel

With the Wailaki, he swam the Eel, rimmed
by fir, the waters bleached by clay bubbling
from cold below—my brother, the white boy.
Stripped, they swam the waters our ancestors
the fish still swim and spawn each year,
they swam, the limbs splashing,
their ribs like fingers gripping cargoes of air.
When the river froze, the Sinkyone boys
peeled off their shoes, fled the schoolhouse,
skating the ice in their leathery feet.

They climbed the outcrop of granite that made
the river bend; with *"Geronimo,"* they
clutched their knees and cannon-balled over
the deepest spot, sinking down into dark.
Then they climbed out of the water, and sat
on the muddy banks, filled their lungs, chests
rising to palaces of air—as one—
Sinkyone, he, and Wailaki, too—
singing a hymn to the summer starlight.
For by then night lay on the river bend.

Uncle

The shy one, Nell's help and stable boy,
braved the Eel in a dory
when spring came, and dredged the sightless
depths for pipes frozen since Christmas—
last on the line of the yellow bus,
skidding through slush
to Branscomb in a downpour.
Stony Nell waited by the door.

Grown, he shipped to Copenhagen.
Father dead, Nell traded
home for acreage in mangoes,
plums and new-fangled tangelos.
Plump Santa Rosa plums he loved best,
but soured his face whenever addressed—
pursing his lips and making tough
as anyone does who's had enough.

Two Crops
(2000)

Along with the tar weed
sticking to the ox's rump,
the Branscombs traveled
north toward the Lost Coast
from the Mayacamas.

They took hold in the land,
its folds and creases
rumpled as a man's shirt
laundered in rain water
and dried in the sun.

They stayed a hundred years.
With the grass that traveled
with them taking root
in the fields, their kids fed
the goats, bedded the hens.

This spring, the one crop
reseeded once more in
the good Branscomb soil.
The other's plowed deep
under the graveyard
weeded now by goats
gone wild, under the oaks
where four hens are brooding.

Trionesta

"I was the world in which I walked"

—*Wallace Stevens*

Water froze in the walled cistern,
fir boughs leaned on drums of rye,
fir tops spiking the air.
Even fences seemed to murmur.
Fire burned, embers
stirred in the crumbling chimney.
You slept on, as did the daubers,
child prone on your knee.
You dreamt of far-off places.
Wind whistled in the pear trees
rattling the pantries.
Foxes tripped your snares.
You flew down the lanes,
sulfurous, scabby towns,
memory terrain,
the world your wedding gown.

Your child, my mother, pillowed
with insects hatching in the staves
whenever the heat waves
swelled up and down the corn rows.
Fearless of marsh hawks,
beetles, rattlers, and bees, she napped
among cattle and cornstalks,
till the drowsy sun slept.
I've never been to Branscomb,
or slept in fir boughs by a lane.
So little changed!
Everywhere you looked was home.
Yet I know, as my mother

knew, those lanes stifling as corn rows,
you at the core in all weather,
no matter the times or the boroughs.

Out of Reach

We walked through tall grass
the hares nested in,
burrs sticking to our hems
as we crossed the orchard
littered even then with plums.

We could still hear our father
on the porch, his voice rising
into leafy oaks, towering
in the dusk, and Mother's
answering murmurs.

If Father called out then,
urging us back from the dark,
his voice was lost, for by then
we'd climbed to the soda springs,
and drifted beyond his reach.

Now you are both gone; yet
your voice is still with me
as I make my quick way
up Branscomb Road once more
by the thickening brambles.

You follow like my shadow,
though your gravestone's just here,
in sight of the western sea
down this narrow road; and
here's our father's, too, beneath
the scraggly, broken plum tree.

That spring day

(Branscomb 1920)

we went from Corning
to Jackson Valley,
the young ones talking
city jobs, heady
new starts. I was seeing
a future cloudy
and cramped as the wide
river met the salt tides.

At Branscomb we never
stood on ceremony—
life was somehow larger
than that. Chaste or cocky,
one by one the older
ones, their energy
fierce, went on their way
just as we had in our day.

I knew the westering
days were gone,
hidden from sight like tree rings.
I would be left alone
by my children, left behind
like the Platte, the Shoshone,
like Devonshire,
the old maps and guides.

For some of the others
everything they sought
was theirs, as first comers.

Whenever I could, I fought
like Coho spawning up river
to maintain the family plot
at this, the end of our line.
For this I saved my dimes.

In the Pear Orchard

(1915, 1968)

As I'm walking an evening,
a hulk veers my way. I pause,
and stiffen rather than punch
in self-defense or raise my knee —
I'll tighten my thighs, and push on:
'Don't you mess with me.'
I train in small steps, my tread
old Chinese. I bind my forehead
like a Jew, and learn to read
sounding out each word,
my progress slow—though, granted
life's wild moments occur—

The day you led a young
girl to the orchard below
the big house, she gave herself to you.
I was conceived. In one afternoon,
three destinies were made among
the rotting pears of autumn.

Dialogues

(Nell, 1975)

1

All summer the wild rose bloomed,
sweet juice of the raspberry
ran under the redwoods where
you children grew, rattling me
with our questions, always more
questions: 'How are babies born?'
'How did the universe start?'
As a girl, I was denied
the liberty of questions;
now I answered when I could—
never about my girlhood,
in distant Erie, P.A.—
from that I turned away—
but much on weeding the garden
beets, broccoli and cauliflower,
on rolling out flaky crusts
for meat pies baked in the wood
stove from the sheep we raised and
slaughtered in the back acre.
To all our mystic longings,
our working hands make answer.

2

"Don't go to the river"—warning
you ignored, for the river,
the spur of the Mattole, moved out
and away from Bear Creek ranch,
and carried spawning Coho,
finger-fished by ten-year olds
who strutted home with dinner.
Grown at last, you left, taking
my answers and leaving me
withered beside the wild rose,
raspberries, my hands idle—
weeping as I'd never wept,
remembering how my head
ached from the blows to my ears,
how my hands burned in the cold.
I longed to ask you how that
could be, me a child, cutting
ice way down in Lake Erie
to haul uphill to the big
orphan-house kitchen in town,
but I couldn't form the words.

Gwen

Nellie's daughter Gwen was wooed by a lumberjack and
ran away with him when she was still a teenager, never to
return. Yet in running away, she seemed to leave most of
herself behind, like silt from a flash flood emptying the
creek's waters willy-nilly into the sea. The colors of the
new life had no time to dry on the canvas before she was
off, moving again into a new day. Gwen's mother drove a
horse drawn wagon to the house where her children would
be born. Gwen sat beside her new husband in a gleaming
Chevy, and soon, soon, they would be flying, leaving the
earth behind in small patches of color.

Artemis in the Barnyard

(1940)

She didn't hear the gate in the flurry
of hens, squalling, stretching out their necks,
checking for foxes one second, the next
pecking nuggets of millet and barley
hidden in the wood shavings, then stiffening
their plumes again in fright. She didn't hear
the gate's click, the man slipping in, daring
to gaze on her—the oval of her face,
the halo of ruddy hair, her legs splayed,
her axe raised high over the waist-high stump.
But just as her axe reached the pinnacle
of its arc, she felt his presence; as he
turned to go, her wedge finished its arc, she
severed the neck of the Plymouth Rock—
white plumes going Mars red on bloodied oak.

She had scared him off; he wouldn't return.
She turned to the work at hand and when
that was done, still thinking of him, she went
down to the barn where the millet was stored.
Lifting up her yellow apron as if
to rescue overripe plums from their tree,
she bent over the millet bin and scooped
an apron of seed with her thoughts of him.
These she scattered to the Plymouth Rocks.
The rest she sowed; it prospered in her fields.
In the hills and river banks of Branscomb,
she grew famous for her hens whose eggs she
sold in the General Store on Branscomb Road.
Even now, standing in her fields under
a rising moon, she hears someone sighing.

Branscomb Road

I took my bride away from
Branscomb town, the barnyard's
tempo; just past Cloverdale,
we eased onto the highway
rubbing the spine of the West.
LA to Vancouver we
took the curves, racing horses
of Apocalypse. Never
again did we walk alone
on Branscomb Road together—
instead, we grew wings, buntings
in streaks of color, making
nests of dried grass and old leaves.
Our young flew and so did we
leaving youth on the shoulder
where plastic blooms mark the rim.
We scorned the pace of idlers
in armchairs, sluggards under
the winter oaks, the earth where
she lies now in endless silence.

Main Street

As the Coho swimming the Eel,
naked she came into the world
breathing an air dissolved in words,
growing up reedy and pale
in the hills above a homestead,
her people saying what they thought,
often not much, the day's work,
predictions of weather and ache.

She helped her father in the store,
though there weren't many customers,
weren't many of any kind, days
long, as they swept, dusted and stocked
the shelves or simply stood staring
at the one street, Main Street, talking
up and down the town's business,
in and out of whatever passed.

Habit of talk sustained living,
held off boredom, till one evening
things took a turn, as they're apt to,
and a man came down the post road,
handsome, not taciturn, but bold,
and off they sallied together
far as his faraway province,
his township of war and dalliance.

Gwen
(1955)

Slender, pale, auburn-haired,
on the night of her wedding
she encountered a certain
sorrow she'd not met in the leas
below the soda springs
of the Northern Wailaiki.
Long married, each December
or late in some Novembers,
she took the Chevy outbound
like a Missus Van Winkle
to the summer fairgrounds,
stiffly prinked in her best suit,
and everywhere she traveled,
looked for herself, searching
all the Union Square shops
with their expensive wrappings
and their brisk, lean sales clerks
murmuring in French-Italian.
Her slender figure's mirrored
in the tall glass, distinctly—
she's just now slipping between
the rich changing room brocades,
trying on a silk chemise,
then a satin, a fine tweed,
deep in the Brothers Magnin.
Nineteen blocks to the north, fog,
heavy, pale, and cold, is doing
its slow ghost dance toward her,
toward the delta's silted waters
where the wintering Chinook
once flashed out of the wide sea,
hook-jawed salmon, their bones
scattered in the preserving sea.

Interstates

Circling bright cities, we arc,
crisscrossing the curve of water
or swooping down the ramp
from 101 to 80,
our coursing, blinking lanes
leading one to another
like veins pulsing with blood.
Night transforms us. Travelers
become stars shooting low
on the skyline, lost to
themselves, to the others
speeding by in the dark—
high beams on dim, racing
mile by mile to find
the wet pavement, the black
macadam, soft and hot.
Bound together, we rush
like falls of water, as one,
accomplishing our arc
by instinct, through pure drive.
On and on, we travel,
the Earth unfolding along
its seams of rock and soil;
we score the ground as we go,
not knowing whether we're
coming now or going.

Herring Gull Variations

(Bodega Bay 2005)

In brilliant crest and spotted bill,
he swiveled, darting me a look,
and skimmed out over the swell.
In my wide scarf and canvas shoes,
I had—he saw—far too much bulk
to ride with him, and so he flew.
  He lacked legs to skulk.

I admired his skill and nerve.
He would not soon come back to me
to perch along the rail; he'd veer
off from one with my plain address,
wild thing rising above a sea
vast now in smooth marine largess.
  No matter he thieved—

as did another on the pier,
his hands not stopping their flutter,
sifting through the midden there.
Oily, matted hair, scabby skin,
red eyes. Did we know each other?
"Lost," I thought, but I knew in him
  a fellow traveler.

III

Hills above the Eel

The father

The father becomes the grandfather, who may become if
he is lucky, the great-grandfather, generation to generation.
In the 20th Century, certain patterns repeat from the 19th:
Brothers go far from home; sisters endure very different
fates; strangers come among us, whom we take as our
own. Constantly we struggle to make a living, bear our
children, understand the mysteries of the nature and its
workings in us, endure the pain and dislocation of growing
old, appreciate the release of death. We have new roads to
travel, or the same road to travel again. We set out, and we
return, the road winding away to the horizon, waiting, we
have the setting sun.

> Our forms, slow to change, repeat:
> Cupid, clown, bully, deadbeat,
> paragon, puck, prince, pauper,
> madman, maid, thief, marauder,
> featherbrain, hero, fisherman, father.

Another Eden

Another, forgotten Eden
had no Tree of Knowledge until two
lithe creatures looked at one another,
and words sprang to their lips, Man, Woman,

the name of elemental oaks,
the grass beneath their feet, the gingko
on the hill, the willow by the creek,
toward evening, the name for cold.

While one named their silence and fear,
the other named the dark, the bones.
Beyond the glen lay evergreens; there
they named the pine, fir and pinions.

They said mine, yours, anger, pain,
and from these a world began.
Fire, they said, and fire cleared the land
and wheels turned and ground the grain.

They slept side by side under the trees,
forbidding nothing, discovering
sweet ease, urgency, discovering
the smooth workings of their bodies.

Rains came and washed the earth; a river
parted them, she on one side, he on
the other. Adam, she said. Eve, he
said. They slept as the spirit moved them

till effaced with all the rest by the sun.
They did not decamp this Eden.

Paper Route

(Berkeley, 1933)

The bay's un-spanned and open
the year he swings off the stair
onto the narrow street that bends
to these cold, Pacific waters.
Cloud banks rise west and hover.
He's carefree, glad to be moving,
to be off in a whirlwind.

Rain or shine, he's off somewhere,
pumping hard, hunching his torso,
splitting the November air,
a falcon, a sharp, small
wedge of brown worsted wool.
Gravel clatters against steel
as he veers and skids on the hill.

The father he'll later become—
even from here I see his aura—
driven, yet puzzled in the end.
What happiness in racing away
to the far places he'll attain!
Still, he only really found himself
at the slow, lowly turtle's pace.

The Full Monty

It was after the War when he learned to fly
that he came to be called the Full Monty,
yet another wild plainsman to hurry
his Cessna pony for a view, bird's eye,
of doings below the white clouds. Gadfly
of the high corn rows, he buzzed the shanties
on the Eel and Russian where the dollies
he once loved sat splay-leg in their lanais.
He rode alone down the dry arroyos,
bucking the bronco of buffalo clouds,
till looking to go aground of zion,
he ground his teeth, brought down the nose
(but not the landing gear) where rye lay plowed
among the hay bales southeast of Eden.

Meditation on flying

1

The Wrights crossed the Ohio and stopped—
not plunging on, not seeking to quench a thirst in that
            rutted edge ward trek.
Instead, they turned to shudder of wings,
        blurring feather and bone,
                    tip and whirl.
It happens still on nights
        Adam joins angel, forming girl.

2

                    Daylight.
A well-dressed man, facedown,
nested his hips in a wooden frame,
hands gripping forward-jutting sticks,
well-shod feet braced in a T-bar wired to a
            spiral twist,
hips' swivel full of consequence.

At each open side, they stood
        at the start of something new,
when the prone one, in wild prenuptials, yelled,
            "Let go!" —
rising in the salty breeze.

And the wind was right.
He, too, rose, from the ground:
                he began to fly.

3

Exploring winged form in secret on the dunes
                of the Carolinas,
riding the salty air,
            a seeker of *tao* altered
letter by letter his grammar,
                  twinning a new
being from his ribs, now big as condor wings,
      now monstrous,
                now haunting.

Rising Over California

Cessna humming, he mounted
the air, climbing above a land
once rich, now dusty, in ruins.
Bronco of the clouds, he saw
the land spread out like a strand
of flesh, a woman burning
on her pyre—Shasta and Weed,
Weott, Bear Creek, and Redding.

Once rivers of salmon ran
through stands of redwood timber,
and herds of cattle rumbled
over Humboldt; steamers ran
to the slaughterhouses, some
breaking up on rock or shoal
off Westport or Eureka;
men were shiny bees in swarm.

The Cessna was carapace
as he hummed tunes to the dead,
singing to sleeping guard dogs,
and dipped under rising fog,
scanning the ground below him
for signs of the hill towns once
busy with purpose, searching
the dark for lost mother lodes.

Snake in the Grass

Stretched in the dry grass full five feet,
unmoved by my light step, the snake
has swallowed a furry creature.
Like the viper in Genesis,
later he may slither up an elm
and take a small-prey census,
turning sniper after his meal.
But at this moment, his vision
restricts to grass and the fools gold
flecking the granite beside him.
He does not see himself: he's all tail
bulging where the gray squirrel went.
From my rock, as I look down, snake's
a crevice in the yellowed ground.
How whole he is; nothing janus.
He has no two-ness; he's all One.
Then, perhaps to break with that, put
his self within his range of sight,
his shaft begins to undulate
and spiral like a human mind
that has been struck; he coils to naught,
then signs the infinite
there in the lazy grass of spring.

Awake Now

(Jackson Valley 1935)

The young buck, budding antlers down,
hanging in the oak, will soon be skinned.
Disturbing the cool air, flies swarm.
The Cinderella-girl is bound
to swat them for her father-king.

"Come on," he says, whispering,
his fingers broken. Gretel now,
she rocks back on her heels, sailing
to him, his gravelly voice drawing
her on, an archipelago of sound.

"Bees are here," she says, now Hansel.
He touches his wallet—the pocket
swollen with bills. "Bring a shovel."
But she cups it, still warm, mindful
it might have been her own heart.

Now ants scurry round the blood.
Swift, he strips the buck of skin,
and it sways naked on the cord.
The head—what remains—sniffs the ground
dark with him. She awakens then.

Dog Creek

You were the one favored by the gods
of those days, the one to charge the hill
like a fledgling crow and maraud
the garden, or swing out over
the shingled warrens, rising above
Dog Creek in your tire swing, rising
above us all in that town of sawmills.
I was the twin teased for my cowlicks,
mimicked for my sad look, my tears,
my pigeon toes, for my antics
steady as rain in the Mayacamas
washing off the smell of naphtha.
At school when the sawing began,
you ran up the lane, all unawares.

"Out of the way!" she barked, standing,
her arms akimbo, fat and brown,
and the moldy tree and your swing
came down that windless October noon,
as we all grow cold, late or soon,
leaves pressing the ground like hands,
sky what's left of leafy crown.
The job was finished, buzz saw stilled,
wood stacked by the chimney
before we knew. It wasn't *your* tree till
she saw you standing there. It's true,
she had only meant to spare you
when she ruled, "Go play out back now,"
though that's where Dog ran in its fury.

Dust

I like dust more than knobbly gravel,
more than slivers of oak or prickly
beds of pine needle by the river.
I prefer the Mayacamas' rough
pathways, where tarmac is scarce and dust
seeps under the windows where they crack
and rides brooms of wind down the chimneys.
Dust soaks up sun and cozies with worms.
Dust rises in halos round my feet.
When I come from the river, and stand
shivering under the big pines, it
oozes and froths up between my toes.
My friend will have none of it and frowns
at me through the back kitchen window.
She's my falconer, recalling me
to perch on silk well above such things.
I, too, once yearned for fine tall houses,
and rode on the wind to the parlors.
It's true, I do not love dust more than
the grasses where deer lay down at dusk.
I am the dust lathered to dark mud
by the waters of my home the Eel.

Landscape with Snakes

Our quick-running silver was already
seeping, unseen, back into the slow ground,
closing commerce with the outside, the year
our mother sailed inland on a lotus,
limbs entwined, while her boys went on living
in the long dream of the fathers' fathers
where it was always summer, so it was
late August when we slipped from our cots
beneath the netting of the sleeping porch,
lying under Sanhedrin's shadow, and
swung our rifles up on our shoulders, our
flashlights bobbing in the dark, and parted
the fields of waist-high grass with our thighs
to the edge of the airstrip, where buzzing
like Cessnas above the world, we descended
on brush squats and nests of the cottontails.
Flashing our lights, we spun quick fire into
the soft white fur, and in the spread of blood
became entangled in the fescue grass
of fields our dreamy fathers named Eden.
Rattlers slithered over granite like streaks
of mottled grey light from another world—
we took them for the water of a spring
until heads and tails rose up, framing them—
the wide, wedge-shaped mouths, jointed
rattles dancing like rice-paper, *ts-ka ts,*
ts-ka, as we circled now, fluttery as moths,
while in the summer palace of Sanhedrin,
our mother slept on, coiled in her bed,
and the cold-blooded, at home in Eden,
lay in wait for us, there, among the grasses.

Social Studies

Murmuring of Hiroshima turned to field
of blackened dahlias, Mrs. Lum stood
before the darkened room as light unfurled
like a leaf on the bark of the known world.

Dipping her brush, she'd shown us ideographs
for 'Man' and 'Baby;' restless for recess,
we'd eyed through glass the fields of tall grass
and laughed as our ink ran down the paper.

Then lights dimmed once gleaming on our desks;
thin strips of acetate clicked and skittered
from the mouth of the rattling projector
images at first like her arabesques.

One was black-white shadow—the ullage
of a man, scalage reduced to smudge,
something from Plato's cave pooled out of air
and flashed onto the white stone of a bridge.

Nothing remained of him but the shadow
on that bridge where he had been standing
when Enola droned, clicking and whirring,
splitting the noon sun to pi or zero.

Trees of Harvest

At dusk and again at dawn, a fresh barge
entered the circles of dark-light, fire-glow
made by lumberyards, the solemn, dusty
play-yards of my secret, dreaming child-self.

All along the narrow mountain highways
trees crowded into ghettoes, sequestered,
passive, embracing what they've always been,
scaffold, canopy, the fire-eaten limb.

A piney, pitched wood-scent entered, then,
my word-child being, piercing my skin bark
with the elements of fire, rain, and wind—
a slow-evolving world of leaf and cone.

This world's every present to me, Eros,
sealed in fine tree-rings of viscous resin.
Do you see, love, how I so quickly slip
beneath your bark to the soft, sweet center?

Like the northern forests where I was born,
forests yielding now to our mammoth claims,
I, too, slept standing, my head thrown back,
tilting to the stars, awaiting harvest.

Fire on the Lake

Lake Mendocino
Redwood Valley, California

It's Sunday. Over the fishes,
the lake spreads flat and blue, a spill
of bright color, as noisy boats,
towing skiers, crisscross the water,
their wakes chalk-marking the surface.

Thick nets of brush and yellow grass,
the tinder of fires, hedge the lake.
Shrub-trees climb the steep hills rising
from the shore, and up along the ridge
big, scraggly oaks beard the skyline.

Next valley over, the orchard
pears droop on their stems in the heat.
Any moment the dry brush will flame.
As on a spit, turning, turning,
the bather on the shore browns, burns.

Just down the road, the Reverend Jones
collects tithes, gathers his people.
He kindles their spirit fires,
while here deep under the sizzle,
fish still circle in their Eden.

Trees

Once trees gathered, rushing
up the mountain, pummeling
one another, crowing,
echoing through the canyons;
the laurels of evergreen
crowning the mountains.

They drew lumbermen
who swarmed in denims
on bark, needles and cones,
turning saws like millstones
grinding to dust the grain
where the last cut was made.

Skittered by winch and windlass,
they massed at the river's bend
with the freshwater bass,
met there by truckers who send
their loads to the sawmills
billowing smoke and ash.

So many trees, such presence.
Once, flying five tenths
of a mile above woodlands,
we saw them, freshened
by recent rains. O trees,
running far as eyes can see!

Mendocino Co.

All the towns had millwrights
who tinkered and smoked
where the white pines shone a strange
blue in an angle of light
in the Maacamas Range.
Fourth of July's, they deafened
the air with bangers,
and clenched their pipes when they rived,
so the millhands all listened
whenever the millwright arrived
to tinker the whipsaw vanes,
and tune the pitman
beside the red hot teepees,
where the ties were made for the trains
running by flaming poppies.

Now those domed mills are closed.
The millhands idle
at the inn of Novato;
the millwrights' pipes are cold.
From here, there's nowhere to go.
Come summer, some will glean
the Anjou, spreading
to dry the slivers of pear;
and where they camp, wind will lean
into the pines, stirring the air.
Women will crack walnuts
in their slant huts;
the children run wild, where
sky casts a long, blue gamut
through the Maacamas air.

Exile

(1964)

1

Father and I sat on cushioned seats
listening to the rain, a fire
crackling when Father looked at me,
and broke the news, "Your Ma and I . . ."
Like stone or ice we sat staring,
as the fire smoldered to ash. Come
dawn, I would be sent away.
That household in chaos, Father's
trigger finger near exploding
his own garrulous, gaping mouth—
then, snap, all was settled—I'm bolting
to live in some dark tower
in deep woods before winter has ceased.
So I went as time does toward
Father's roads, bedrocks under me,
my way as ordained and drunken
as any birthing or flying,
foolish and lost, inching along
from day to day, soaring, stumbling.
This tower ever cossets me,
this round room no one may enter.
Companions shuttered to me, I
keep my solitary chamber;
my tap-tapping in that circuit
a kind of walking in the mind,
shopping round and round the market
for *alephs*, picking out the rhymes.

2

By that time I'd grown more akin
to the reedy throated owl, ghostly
flitting through the woods off Laurel,
slipping through the dark
into the woods for sleep—
the seeds of this planted long ago
in the hard chert of the Maacamas.

My pocket was a street warren
of shacks and wolves sewn by a Ma
undone by my plunge from her womb.
I sought my Messiah on strolls,
in the tall, white Arabian
standing in his field of fescue,
in the oak crowning our flat house.

I did not find Him anywhere,
but for awhile, I was no more
the least child, I was *first*, spinning
as I pleased past feeling, flesh, grit,
past the rattler curled in a jar
in the pale green light of the porch.

Father Oak and Mother Bramble,
MacKerricher, north, Westport, south,
Ten Mile, Abalobadiah,
these were my first coordinates,
Grit and ash, flour, bone, dust and meal—
mad shouts, nothing is turned away—
from these I built my tower.

Eclipse

At dawn, the house begins to stir.
Rising wind tugs strings of pollen
through the spring dark; taping the bare
magnolia branches, they beckon.
Someone's in the kitchen, humming
as she works, scrubbing pots, sipping
coffee; to clatter of saucers,
I slip out, sack on my shoulder.
The streets call to me, and I go
down into the crowded hovels,
their roofs littered with pine needles,
with leaves of magnolia and oak.

I follow the tarmac seaming
the old neighborhoods; strolling
walkways just as day begins,
I pass trees scented in lemon.
I pass my library of Proust,
O'Hara and Melville, and the hut
of the lonely stranger, the arbors
of his furtive love, the vendors,
the windows blossoming cowslips
the fields in purple iris:
every one in constant eclipse
in the heart's recording office.

Ode to a Sprinkler

We laugh out loud in joy
to find the old sprinkler
at the back of the highboy
in our attic's lair.
Boy of action, you spear
its metal stake and screw it
hose-end to the gnarled faucet.

At first, it mists the air
bejeweling pots of fern
but with a flick of wire,
a fresh, full spray arcs
out, piping instant glamour
to the grassy swatch immured
by beech, dogwood, and fir—

Happy as Buddhas,
we sit in the heat—
assigning to another era
beyond our childish glee
the rain, the wells of sweet
water in the inner realms
of stone-forming earth.

For rain falls at our command
in the sprinkler's swish, swish
in this desert kingdom,
and we skate the surface
held by its tension,
and share with air a pressure
equal in measure.

Earthquake Weather

(2001)

Over the Maacama,
storm clouds touch down on the hills
mottled as snake skin with cinnabar,
bluecrist and color of jade.
Creviced stands of pine form dark swathes
like sweat in the sleeping canyons—
the heat's that strong today,
the wind hot, everything dry.
I can see to the valley,
its floor a flat-bottomed boat—
mills and houses and two men
against a truck, one of them—
dark, keen—might be my father.
Desultory, they smoke and talk,
shuffling and raising clouds of dust
mingling with the smoke of pipes—
insignificant, really,
to the billowing mill smoke,
hardly anything at all
to the clouds plowing the air,
nothing at least to me now.
Yet I might move from this heat
into cooler shades below
and stand with him where he smokes—
this small, dark man who more than
once spared me from consequence,
interceding on my behalf
before the gods, before the wrath
of Maacama cooking.

Cochrane Street

Bent, he sidled from room to room,
crammed full of unopened cartons.
Ten feet down he dug the trenches
years ago to irrigate a rose,
and still they crisscrossed the backyard
of the little house on Cochrane.
He carried the old village genes,
the elders' latter day resolve,
but the sense of ancestral time
flowing through him had been broken
by hard times that drove the children
like a blade through a plowed field.
So word would not get out of his
death, his imminent escape,
he told no one, not even me,
but toward the end hobbled three miles
cross town to the county clinic,
staggering into reception,
unshaven, but clean. Wasn't there
a son once, an adopted child
lost in time? He did not appear.
In that village of five hundred,
in due time, his old mother heard
the news and brought a special bed
for his dying to her spare room,
but he wept, begging to go home
to Cochrane Street where a broken
dryer sat out front, a stone's
throw from an abandoned sawmill.

Crow

Now comes a being like me who does not hold,
émigré of inland fields who plunges
aslant the airy threshold
where sea gulls skirr and wild seas beckon;
she dives and swoops over the almonds
rock hard in the purple cold
of autumn; she scavenges

cleverer by half than all the seabirds
patrolling round their swath of sand.
Marauder, blackbird, beggar
she finds the cones and almonds here too bare
but knows fields abroad that bear
for her, and shoots up, landward,
scouting the juicy croplands.

The wind goes on lashing the groves that bend
away from the wide silver-green ocean.
Crow's gone now; only gulls span
and circle this cuff of land, stone binding
the fissures, the tides grinding
the river stones to sand
in long spiraling motions.

Visiting the County Jail

Pale child with strands of oily hair,
girl wild as brambles, "turned out," scared,
rasps and snuffles, shuffling splayfeet
along the penal grit and heat.
Metals clang, echo: the cell's set,
another afternoon ill lit.
This one knows just how high is done,
luck of the draw in coming down,
without ideas of how to quit.
Plexiglas divides where we sit,
she, sullen. Whatever ails her,
she sniffs and picks at her fingers—
after all, she's just seventeen—
and slumps when I ask, "Tell me please,
in your town did any one ask,
'Do you take in the risks of this?'
Or, 'Hey, where will you sleep tonight?'
Just, 'Do you want another hit?'"

For kids like her, there's not much here
but the fields of tall grass and firs
and spotted milk cows taking hold
by rocky outcrops, and foxholes.
People still drop by evenings,
or tour round in season, calling
on other tribes, checking on traps
too often empty, as lapsed
bans and Gallo wine turn men
idle in towns beyond Marin.
Half century on, the roads still run
by stony creeks and green summits
through hills rolling north in the rain.

The double lanes arc where peahens
roost on guardrails; the smooth tarmac
stripes ahead, Indian gold on black.
The Lexus purr by, in no time
passing on, swilling the fields of grain.

Hills above the Eel

Once when we were young, our mother
sent us out of the kitchen,
so west we climbed to the madrones
making their sparse stand on the hill,
and to the old cemetery.

It was country I never had
a hold on, at least not then, and
soon would leave, while he—he stayed on
in those yellow hills by the Eel
where we walked that Thanksgiving day.

Live, he planted, built, and pottered about,
brooding and boozing, stonewalling
his foes and stockpiling antique
arrows he sifted from the Eel
running black and shiny below.

Of many beings, who was he?
A tribal chieftain? He baffles
my desire to capture him and
scatters this memory to air
high above the slow winding Eel.

On a ridge above the river,
it is I now who remain, who
scatter him, ash-light, plain as grief.
Even so he is the one who
lives on here in hills by the Eel.

San Francisco Evenings

Have we gone astray
to live in this ancient place
at strand's end,
where night sews his pocket endways
along the hills?

At dusk the bridge slips
and sails away, a sun-tinged ship.
Lost a moment,
she reappears, regal,
masts of coral.

Here comes my daughter;
we take our meal together
before night echoes
day's end, and at the piano
she taps out a poem.

Time on, silence follows,
memories flock like sparrows,
thoughts tangle.
Has breaking my vows un weighed me,
or blocked my way?

Ships pass—ghostly, unreal.
Like wisps of fog, my people
turned from home,
crossing the mountains for Eden,
an earthly genome.
At first, she didn't grasp

my footnote to our maps,
for me, so visceral:
How settlers shed cradles, cauldrons
on the Plains to Oregon
lightening their struggle.

Walking in Humboldt Co.

Old woman now she retraces
her steps along paths she must have known
a long time ago to feel how
they bend in green fir
to form her solitude, and now
return to her—

manzanita below a peak,
tree limbs moaning as if to break,
shutters banging, remnants of speech,
flash of berry.
Like brambles, thoughts untangle at the creek.
Travel-weary

she moves on through waist-high cresses,
Mendocino sedge and grasses,
toward a patch of brambly posies,
not far from death,
and smells one last time the wild roses.
They pierce her breath.

Zara Raab grew up north of San Francisco to parents whose own great-grandparents settled in Northern California in the 1800s. She attended high school in Portland, and then Mills College in Oakland and graduate school at the University of Michigan. In Ann Arbor, she earned at Master's in philosophy, but continued to write and publish poems. She lived in Paris, and supported herself as a freelance writer in Washington, D.C. and later in San Francisco. In the early 1980's, she took the name Zara Raab, and once her children were raised, she began publishing poems and reviews in earnest. Her poems appear in *West Branch, Arts & Letters, Nimrod, The Dark Horse, River Styx, Crab Orchard Review* and elsewhere. Her literary reviews and essays appear in many small magazines, including *Raven Chronicles, Poet Lore, Boxcar Review,* and *Colorado Review.* She lives in Berkeley, California.

CPSIA information can be obtained at www.ICGtesting.com
Printed in the USA
269388BV00001B/6/P